POLIO
and
PTSD

One Person's Struggle with and
Triumph over the Psychological Damage
of A Major Childhood Illness

Charlene Elizabeth

ISBN: 978-1-4834-9827-0 (sc)
ISBN: 978-1-4834-9826-3 (e)

Library of Congress Control Number: 2019902420

Lulu Publishing Services rev. date: 03/26/2019

DEDICATION

To all persons who had polio, their families and friends, and to all interested health care professionals. The World Health Organization estimates that there are one million polio survivors still living today in the United States, and a total of ten million world-wide.

I hope my story will be of help.

Charlene Elizabeth
Charlotte, North Carolina

Fall of 2018

ACKNOWLEDGMENTS

The statement below is one of an almost record number of heart-warming responses to my March of 1987 paper posted last winter on Facebook's private site, Post-Polio "Coffee House," entitled, "UNFINISHED BUSINESS, Support Group Members Confront Feelings Surrounding the Late Effects of Polio" :

> "It's like someone just reached into my chest, grabbed my heart with their hands, squeezing it, while touching my soul, reaching into the depths of my mind, then wrote out everything I could never say or explain to anyone. Yes, this is a homer into my very being. The pain is real."
>
> Lora Duguay

Thank you to all the polio survivors, and to others, who have encouraged my writing both now and in the past. It gives me the motivation I needed to tell my personal story.

Special thanks to Sabrina Molden, PhD., who guided me through the angst of baring my soul.

To Melanie Lee and the late Joseph Henry Sharp, author-friends, who helped me during the writing and publication of this book, each in their own way.

To Danielle Latoni, OTR/L for her computer expertise.

And, to my parents who gave me what they had to give.

CONTENTS

PROLOGUE

"If you bring forth what is within you, what you bring forth will save you. If you do not bring forth what is within you, what you do not bring forth will destroy you."

Jesus, The Gospel of Thomas

I have spent most of my adulthood bringing forth what was so carefully buried, boarded up, and nailed down, as a child.

This book is not intended to be a complete autobiography, rather one large strand in the braid of my life. Regrettably, many things have been left out in the interest of focusing on one major theme — my experience with polio, primarily the emotional/psychological. That has in large part made me who I am today.

I also want to capture on paper my struggles and my victories, so they will not be lost in the shuffle of time. And, so that my family, friends and my descendants will better know just who I am. It has been said that, "When a person dies, a library burns."

*   *   *

I can't remember a time when I didn't love fairy tales! As a child, hanging on the wall above my bed was a large, framed map of Fairy Tale Land, in color. It had castles, bridges, deep forests, and other symbols of all the well known fairy tales. When I grew up I wrote my own fairy tales about myself, "The Little Lame Princess" and "The Girl Who Had No Skin." (They can be found in the back of this book.) And recently I read three books about the meaning of fairy tales and how valuable they can be, written by three psychiatrists: *Women Who Run With the Wolves* by Clarissa Pinkola Estes; *The Uses of Enchantment* by Bruno Betelheim; and *The Wounded Woman* by Linda Schierse Leonard. We must see to it that children today know these stories. They introduce our little ones to the great drama and themes of life in terms they can understand and yet not be traumatized by.

One fairy tale seems especially appropriate to this book, although there are others, the one about Bluebeard. In his castle there were many doors. His bride was forbidden to enter one of those doors in particular. But while he was away, she unlocked the forbidden door. What did she find? A room filled with bones, blood and skulls! When Bluebeard returned and discovered what his bride had done, he made plans to kill her. However, her brothers came galloping to the rescue and they killed Bluebeard!

This is the story of my opening that door what I found, and of my rescue.

PART ONE

*"The past is never over.
It's not even past."*

———————————

William Faulkner

ONE

Shattered

I felt like a fine piece of crystal hurled against a brick wall! I slid, shattered and sobbing onto the kitchen floor of my straw-bale house where I now lived alone in the mountains of New Mexico. I had been sorely betrayed by a small group of good friends. I began having visions of lying in my coffin, buried deep in the ground.

My therapist diagnosed me with PTSD (Post Traumatic Stress Disorder) soon after.

I didn't believe her!

TWO

In the Beginning

> "In the Spring of my eighth year,
> My soul received a wound so deep,
> That 'though I am recovering,
> I shall always weep!"
>
> Charlene Elizabeth

It all began one lovely Spring morning in a midwest city in 1943. I was eight years old. The birds were chirping and the sun was smiling as I sprang from my bed to get my doll. It was the last time I would ever spring anywhere! My right leg folded beneath me and I collapsed on the floor. I yelled for my mother.

The next thing I remember was lying on a gurney in a hospital hallway. A nurse was saying to my mother, "Oh, what a beautiful child! It's a shame we didn't get her sooner!" I HAD POLIO!

I had been having pain for several weeks in my neck, back and legs. Our family doctor was away in World War II. The doctor filling in for him told my parents it was just "growing pains." Amazing, since there were a number of polio cases in our area at the time and a cousin of mine in the South had had polio, yet my parents had accepted the doctor's diagnosis.

The hospital was a small, one-story facility just for the contagious diseases so prevalent among children then. It has long since been torn down and replaced by an automobile dealership. All the records which were kept in the basement in cartons, destroyed.

I was put in isolation at once, a room by myself, of course. I was contagious. I could have no visitors, there were no telephones in the patient's rooms, and television was non-existent. Any books or toys I might have would need to be sterilized and therefore ruined, when I was eventually moved to a ward. My beloved grandparents were allowed to stand in the hall outside my door on Sunday afternoons, the only visiting day. They thoughtfully brought homemade grape juice, popcorn and the funny papers each time they came. My father brought a step ladder to my window and visited with me that way.

I was given a blood transfusion and had an indescribably painful spinal tap. I was afraid. I knew people died of polio. The intense pain continued in my muscles. Those in my back were so contracted, the nurse could easily slide both her hands beneath me. Things weren't looking good.

In an instant, I had been taken away from everyone and everything I had ever known with no preparation, explanation or support. This is how I learned that the world is not always a safe or fair place, that physicians, parents and prayers can't always fix things. Hospitals then were cold, rigid Victorian places. There was no one I could talk with, no social workers, no psychologists yet.

In Clark Moustakas's book, *LONELINESS,* he states, "The possibility of being abandoned or left alone is the most serious threat to a child's whole existence. Of the many kinds of temporary abandonment, no experience is more desolating to a child than having to be in a hospital alone … terrifying fear, anxiety and traumas survive long after the physical defect has been rectified."

In *STRESS, LOSS and GRIEF,* psychiatrist and internationally known authority on the topic, John Schneider, tells us, " …when a serious loss happens to a young child it is more devastating than for adults because a child hasn't yet formed an adequate world-view and is therefore apt to assume things she/he cannot check out." Polio strikes at a very vulnerable age. I cried myself to sleep every night, with my head under my pillow, fearing a scolding from the staff. I taught myself to cry without making a sound. Thus, I began to stuff my feelings and I developed a pattern that would continue for years.

I understand that many children hospitalized with polio were scolded and/or punished for crying. One very sad example is a two year old boy, in the hospital for an entire year. His parents lived too far away to visit often. He cried. He cried for his mother. He cried when cockroaches invaded his crib at night. A nurse would push his crib into the linen closet, turn out the light and lock the door until he stopped. He grew up to be a man full of rage. Eventually he killed himself. With a gun.

During the weeks I was in isolation I heard not one word from my mother! No cards or letters with comforting messages, no treats or little presents left at the nursing station, no stepladder visits at my window. As a mother and grandmother, I am appalled! Dear God! Did she think children didn't have feelings, had no understanding of what was going on? I was completely abandoned by her in my time of greatest need.

THREE

Polio Facts & Questions

For those who don't know, polio, poliomyelitis, or infantile paralysis, as it is also known, is a virus that attacks the central nervous system, mainly in children, sometimes young adults. It often causes permanent paralysis, breathing problems and even death. It has been around for a long time; there is evidence of polio in Ancient Egypt. Today, fortunately, polio has been irradicated in many parts of the world, thanks to the vaccines developed by Dr. Jonas Salk and Dr. Albert Sabin in the 1950's, and the more recent campaign conducted by the Rotary Club to vaccinate every one everywhere.

It is nearly impossible for those persons born after the vaccines to imagine, the fear, the heartbreak and damage of those times. It was worse than the AIDS epidemics because it is more contagious. President Roosevelt declared war on polio and founded the March of Dimes which was established to collect funds for combating this dread disease.

Many polio survivors today have been experiencing new physical problems after years of stability, and to their great dismay. These new problems include new pain and weakness in the muscles, joints and nerves, unusual fatigue, and sensitivity to the cold. Ever competent and industrious, many people who had polio began organizing, with the help of health care professionals, to address these issues and related matters.

I have wondered many times why I contracted polio when my sibling did not, nor did my playmates and classmates. "To contract" is an interesting verb often used when speaking of contagious diseases. A contract is an agreement between two or more parties. Did I agree to have polio at some level of consciousness, or was my immune system low? I was sick a lot in early childhood with whooping cough, chicken pox and measles, plus numerous bad colds, sinus infections and stomach flu. I spent a lot of time in bed. Could my low resistance possibly have been due to the stress in my family? It's a fact that there is a strong mind-body connection.

It was no secret among our family and close friends that my parents had a highly troubled marriage. My father was prone to tempestuous explosions and my mother to major crying spells. Our home life was usually in emotional turmoil and I was the designated peacemaker. One evening at dinner, I must have been seven or eight, my mother who never raised her voice, stood and yelled down the table at my father, "I want a divorce!" I instantly shot out of my chair, ran to the bathroom in the back of the house, climbed on the toilet seat and went out the window, hiding in the back yard. Television's Dr. Phil often says that children should not be burdened with adult problems. So true. Did I contract polio to keep my parents together? A haunting question. If so, I succeeded! They slogged through a total of thirty-five years before my father died of colon cancer. Did he carry his anger in his gut?

I'll never know the answers to these questions, but I did read of a doctor who was researching why some communities had polio epidemics and others did not, why some cities seemed predisposed. I never heard of the conclusions he reached, if any, but the fact that he was asking those questions still interests me.

Richard L. Bruno, H.D. PhD., says in his book, *The Polio Paradox, What You Need to Know*, "that … emotional injury — stress— is known to suppress the immune system, causes the release of a variety of hormones and has also been suggested to increase susceptibility to all infections."

FOUR

Confined

"The game of life. You never know how hard it will be. You never know when it will end. You can't control it. You can only adjust."

Angel Nava Lopez

When beyond the contagious stage of polio, I was moved into a ward of girls and a young woman who was in an iron lung. The patient in the bed next to mine was Kay. She had been a next-door playmate when we were pre-schoolers, then her family moved across town. We got sick at the same time, but couldn't have gotten polio from each other several years later. It helped to have her company again. I would spend the next six months confined to a space about the size of a child's grave, except for physical therapy treatments down the hall. I did request permission for an overnight pass on Halloween so I could go home and see the trick-or-treaters' costumes when they came to our front door. My request was granted.

We all underwent Sister Kenny treatments in that hospital, consisting of being wrapped in hot, wet woolen packs cut from Army blankets then covered with pieces of plastic shower curtains to keep in the heat and moisture. When the packs cooled down, they were replaced, all day, every day except Sunday, visiting day. The cooling wool itched and scratched.

This through the hot, humid dog-days of a Michigan summer. There was no such thing as air conditioning.

It was unbearable at times and I got through it, I think, by mentally detaching from my body and overriding the misery — coping mechanisms that became entrenched and would work to my detriment in later years when faced with other problems. The Sister Kenny treatments were necessary, of course, and most beneficial in that they prevented permanent contractions of the affected muscles and I am very grateful for that.

In the evenings we shed our G-strings and put on our pajamas. We often played catch, throwing any handy object from bed to bed. A gift from my Aunt Frances, I had on some p.j.'s made of a new fabric called *nylon*. It was being used in place of silk for parachutes during the war. It didn't breathe and was very slippery. One night, during a game of catch, I accidentally slid right out of my bed and onto the floor which was considered highly contaminated. In my mind, landing on the floor was the equivalent of a lethal dose of radiation today! I was terrified! Somehow I struggled back into bed using my strong leg, pulled the covers over my head and stayed that way until the next morning. I was fervently hoping a nurse hadn't seen me and that the other girls wouldn't tell. However, no damage was done and no one told. I was a very sensitive and imaginative little person ... qualities that are both assets and liabilities!

A young Catholic priest, new in town, came to see us every Friday, bringing take-out ice cream sundaes for each of us, including the boys in the ward next to us. So, Fridays were days we looked forward to and that priest became an important friend in my adult life.

George had been my playmate and best friend since we were two years old. He lived just down the street from my house. One day his mother brought him to the hospital to see me. He couldn't come inside, but I was taken out in a wheelchair. George performed all sorts of antics on the front lawn to entertain me and make me laugh. Handstands, somersaults, cartwheels. I am still touched by that memory.

My discharge came at last. Wearing only my little white G-string, I stood on newspaper spread on the floor in front of the doctor and my mother, while being evaluated. I could no longer walk. There was obvious damage in my right leg from my waist down to my toes. My leg had become atrophied and I had a drop-foot. I would need a surgeon.

FIVE

Who Will Love Me?

"The greatest trap in our life is not success, popularity or power, but self-rejection."

Henri Nouwen

Back at home in my former world, I threw myself on the couch in our den. I cried. And I cried. And I cried. Even at my young age I knew my life would never be the same again. I wouldn't be like the other girls; boys would avoid me. I was damaged goods, a second, defective and worst of all, I was now unworthy and undeserving of what able-bodied persons could have and be and do. I believed this with all my heart. And so began the serious depression that would plague me off and on for decades.

A wooden wheelchair with a caned back and seat got me around in our house. To go upstairs to my bedroom I had to scoot on my bottom. What did I behold when I got there but a brand new red- and cream- colored Schwinn two-wheeled bicycle, with all the accessories parked at the foot of my bed!! It had been purchased and placed there by my father as an incentive to walk again. What a thrill that was!!

My mother bought books for me, children's classics. I was already a "book worm." She gave them to me one at a time so that each one was special. My favorites were the *Raggedy Ann* and *Raggedy Andy* series and the *Little House on the Prairie* books. I still have those two sets in my bookcase.

One evening my mother sat on the edge of my bed and said, "Now, we're just going to pretend all this (meaning polio) never happened!!?? What?! What was I supposed to do with that?? When there had been all that physical and emotional suffering in the hospital, when I could no longer walk and had major surgeries facing me? Being an obedient child (according to my mother), I went along with it, but it really messed with my mind, my ability to assess reality. Sadly I assumed I had committed some sort of mortal sin that was just too *shameful* to talk about. Friends didn't mention it either Were they afraid of hurting my feelings? Why? Had I done something wrong? My leg became my "*Scarlet Letter*" and there would be no reprieves, no weekend off, no holiday or sabbatical. I would live in the able-bodied world, but I wouldn't really fit in. *Who will love me?*

From what I have since heard, observed and remembered, tragic events were rarely spoken about by anyone in those times. That may have been a way of coping with crises since there were no such people as counselors, psychologists, etc. That is an explanation but I don't consider it an excuse. I am reminded of the extent to which President Franklin D. Roosevelt went to hide his braces and crutches. (No one would vote for a handicapped President!) There exists only one photograph of him in a wheelchair. Society has progressed somewhat since then in that respect. Hopefully, today there are fewer "elephants in the room."

SIX

Operation Detroit

"...courage is not the absence of fear but the triumph over it."

Nelson Mandela

My parents took me to Detroit to see a highly-recommended surgeon, Frank Curtis, MD. He prescribed three surgeries on my foot and ankle: a tendon transplant, an ankle fusion and the severing of a contracted tendon, which all would be done at the Children's Hospital in Detroit.

Being that it was still during the war, gasoline was rationed, so my grandfather volunteered to drive me to the hospital, about seventy-five miles away. He dropped me off in the Admissions Office and picked me up there a week later. I suppose that was standard procedure but I felt more like a bundle of dry cleaning. It must have been as wrenching for my grandfather as it was for me. Again, I was taken from the familiar and put in a strange environment with no preparation or support.

The hospital was located in an old, run-down part of the city. Looking out the window of my hospital room that first night, I saw a tired old man pushing a heavy cart of trash down the street in the darkness. I felt sad for him. I felt very much alone. I remember the line of nursery rhyme characters painted along the top of the walls in my room. They were old and ugly. A nurse took me to a special room and "prepped" me for surgery which was to take place first thing the next morning. She shaved my leg, scrubbed my leg and foot with alcohol, then wrapped them snuggly with long strips of gauze to ensure sterility. I had such a sense of dread in my stomach. I had no idea of exactly what was going to happen to me. I compared it to going to the guillotine. There was no one to hold me, to explain or reassure.

On the operating table the next morning, I was surrounded by big masked men and somehow I knew they had knives. They strapped me down and clamped a sieve of ether over my mouth and nose. I struggled. The ether smelled sweetly sickening. The room began to spin and buzz and I was out.

During that week of surgery and recovery, I received no mail, no calls from home on the nursing station phone. Dear God in Heaven! Is it possible that no one thought children had feelings? Even my father was silent; he couldn't bear the thought of a scalpel being used on "his baby." It seems incomprehensible today!

After recovering for awhile at home, the second operation was performed and it was more involved. It would fuse the bones in my ankle in a way that would prevent a sideways roll. When I regained consciousness, I went through the same wretched nausea and vomiting from the ether that I experienced after each surgery. By nightfall, my foot was throbbing. The plaster cast was too tight around my foot. A nurse called the doctor but nothing could be done until morning. It was a very long night as I sat up in pain. In the morning it was discovered that the resident who put on the cast had done it incorrectly. It would have to be removed and replaced.

They didn't have those small circular saws then. They used something like long-handled stainless steel pruning shears. Starting at the top of the cast and cutting down the outside first, they had to turn the shears at a ninety degree angle at my ankle and right over my tender, new incision. Oh, did that hurt! Another cut was made down the inside of my leg and foot and off came the cast in two half shells and a new cast was put on properly. The skin under a cast would always begin to itch and peel from lack of exposure to the air. One of my grandmother's steel corset stays was just the thing for scratching where fingers couldn't reach.

The third surgery followed in due time. My friend, Kay, was my roommate during the second or third surgery, I can't recall which. Other than that, I went through those operations alone as probably other children did. Unthinkable today.

That summer I was ready to walk again. I was fitted with a brace consisting of two steel up rights, hinged at the ankle, and attached permanently to the bottom of my shoe, with a leather cuff and buckle, just below my knee. My shoes were ugly brown oxfords that laced. Since the brace was fastened to my shoe, I had only the one pair of shoes and had to wear them for dress as well as every day.

I was also given crutches and my grandfather coached me that summer at the lake as I practiced walking again. (My parents and grandparents had rented a cottage together for two weeks in northern Michigan.) One hot afternoon when we were all resting, with the window shades down, I lay on my cot and began fantasizing about getting a butcher knife from the kitchen and harming myself. That was my first suicidal ideation, and not to be my last.

SEVEN

School for the Handicapped

"When we are no longer able to change a situation, we are challenged to change ourselves.

Viktor Frankl

It was time for me to go back to school. I entered fifth grade at a school for handicapped children, having missed most of third grade and all of fourth. Handicapped children were not main-streamed then. Being in a special school meant we could have physical therapy often and during school hours. And the teachers had special training.

There were kids there with all sort of disabilities besides polio, such as a boy with cerebral palsy whose arms and legs flailed in the air when he tried to speak. His parents had moved their family down from the Upper Peninsula of Michigan so he could go to school. A teen-age girl and boy were in my class who were called "blue babies" having been born with inoperable (at the time) heart defects which caused their skin to have a bluish cast along with purple lips and nails. With that disability we all knew they wouldn't live much longer. And, a young girl, born with no neck, who foamed at the mouth and always had a green discharge running from her nose. and many more disfigured children. My heart hurts for them now, but at the time I was mainly horrified that life could be so cruel to its young. My three years at that school were like a bad dream. Again. I wasn't prepared or supported.

We were pushed by the physical therapists, and everyone else, to improve, do better, get back to normal. Their intentions were good, but that likely contributed to the high rate of Type A personalities among polio survivors. We wanted to be like other able-bodied children, only better!! Polio survivors are known to have a higher degree of education and a higher rate employment than any other group of handicappers. We are now faced with the necessity to slow down.

We were picked up and driven to school every morning by a Yellow Cab, and returned home after school by the same cab. This was paid for by the local Rotary Club and was such a helpful service for our parents. Those same Rotarians put on a marvelous Christmas party for us every year at a big hotel, with a big decorated tree and a big Santa Claus. We were asked in advance to submit a list of three items we would most like to receive as a gift. One year I was given a leather portfolio for my music books, with my name embossed in gold; I had begun piano lessons.

Another high spot was when I won a blue ribbon in a dramatic reading contest in the sixth grade. The reading I chose to do was called, "Dark Victory," about a woman who had gone blind. A curious choice. I think I had an attraction to tragedy.

EIGHT

Back in the Mainstream

"You gotta' learn to rise above your raisin'.

Dr. Phil McGraw

Considered ready for the mainstream again, I returned to regular schooling in the eighth grade. I had started kindergarten early and was moved ahead a semester in second grade because school was easy for me. I was now a year younger than my classmates. While I could keep up academically, I was behind in my social development. In other words I was painfully awkward socially. I was also becoming a woman, and boys and girls were beginning to like each other again.

Adolescence was doubly hard for me. I was already just shy of six feet tall, extremely thin, wore glasses which were not a fashion accessory then, and had some of the usual complexion problems. AND I was still wearing my leg brace with the ugly brown oxfords. Girls always wore skirts to school so there was no hiding my leg. I stood out like the proverbial "sore thumb." I was scorchingly self-conscious and avoided all full-length mirrors plus my reflection in store windows. (I still do that.)

Much to my absolute amazement, a boy I had a crush on, who was tall, good looking, smart and popular, invited me to a formal Rainbow/ DeMolay dance! I am sure his mother made him do it, out of kindness, my being new in that school. A first date at age twelve to a formal dance??!!

Of course, I accepted. I happened to already have a lovely soft-red taffeta floor length dress, a worn-once hand-me-down from a distant cousin, whose mother shopped only at the best of stores. The dress had spaghetti straps and a matching short jacket with puffed sleeves. I loved it. I don't remember one thing about the dance itself; I was half sick with anxiety. To this day, I can't stand the fragrance of the cologne I wore.

How did I handle those teenage years under my circumstances? I became a very rowdy tomboy! Loud and boisterous, playing practical jokes both on my classmates and neighbors. I pulled off some real humdingers, I must say. Actually, I was "Laughing on the outside, crying on the inside," Big Time!

During junior and senior high, I attended a private camp for girls in northern Michigan every summer. It was an eight week camp and most of the girls and many of the counselors returned every year, so it was like a second family. My parents made arrangements for me to attend the last four weeks only each summer. The full eight weeks would have been too strenuous. The camp was located on a turquoise-colored lake, surrounded by dark green pines and white birch trees. The camp property had been purchased originally from the Chippewa Indians. This was where, among the beauty of nature, I first *EXPERIENCED* God, as opposed to knowing *about* God.

I recall one summer when there was to be a dance with a nearby boys' camp, to be held at our camp. Our required dress was our "Sunday whites," a white shirt and white shorts, Shorts? I was mortified. The boys would be able to see my leg; they wouldn't want to dance with me. I had just returned from a three day canoe trip and I did my best to feign illness, but the counselors weren't buying it. After much persuading and some compromise, I went to the dance wearing long pants. Except for that dance, that camp was one wonderfully bright spot in my childhood, and I returned for one last summer as a junior counselor. I spent my day off each week sleeping in the infirmary. As a counselor I had to be at camp for the entire eight weeks. That was pushing it.

Senior high wasn't much better than junior high. My dislike for math and lack of aptitude for it kept me out of the Honor Society. I did acquire a group of girl friends I kept in touch with over the years.

I went to the Junior Prom with a boy I'd grown up with, but I felt acutely self-conscious all evening. He told me not long ago that it was one of the five worst events of his life, ranking above Army boot camp!

A friend engineered a date for me for the Senior Prom. I can't recall a thing about the dance, other than what I wore — a white strapless formal purchased in Detroit. Afterwards everyone drove out to the local lovers lane. Still in my formal, my date and I climbed on the back bumpers of the parked cars, jumping up and down and interrupting things. Then we smoked a cigar. I didn't get a goodnight kiss from him until our twenty-fifth class reunion.

*   *   *

After graduation from high school, my parents sent me off to a two year private college for girls in Missouri. That was when I made a conscious decision to become a *lady,* thinking that would make me more attractive to the opposite sex. Early in my second year I received a letter ending a really special summer romance. I was also receiving dire letters from my mother describing her marital misery. I became depressed once more. Not knowing just what to do, I went to see my psychology professor. He suggested I paint a picture of what I was feeling, which I did. It was of a broken tree lying in a clearing in a dark forest. There was a small flower blooming beside the jagged tree stump and a shaft of sunlight focusing on the flower. When I took it back to that professor he was most enthusiastic and said it symbolized optimism. He framed my painting and hung it in his office where it stayed for many years, I am told, and I somehow I managed to go on with my life.

That summer my father arranged a modeling job for me with Oldsmobile, without my knowledge or consent. The photographic shoot was to take place at the local country club. I was to stand beside a Starfire convertible wearing a sweater and Bermuda shorts. Shorts again! I just couldn't do *that!* We were still observing the iron-clad rule in my family about not speaking about my polio so I couldn't talk to my father about it. That would have been yucky!Instead, I called the Oldsmobile executive my father knew, whom I had never met, and explained my situation to him. That in itself was humiliating. But, he already knew and assured me I would be positioned behind a golf bag so my leg didn't show. As it turned out, the Oldsmobile Starfire was discontinued and the photos were never used. That experience still makes me cringe.

Back in college, I met a fraternity man at a mixer at a neighboring university, who was instantly taken with me, leaving his current girlfriend and before long offering me his fraternity pin. His entire fraternity serenaded us one lovely evening in front of the house/dorm I was living in on my college campus. Those male voices were achingly beautiful as they sang, "I Only Have Eyes for You." Of all of my many housemates, I was the only one pinned and serenaded that year. That should have been affirming for me. It wasn't. Eventually I returned his pin, realizing I had just been swept up in the romance of it all. I wasn't really in love or ready to make such a commitment.

After graduating from that college, I transferred to Michigan State for my final two years. My dorm-mates elected me to run in a major beauty queen contest held by the School of Engineering I didn't win, but was a runner-up on the court. About the same time I was invited to join a popular national sorority, although joining a sorority was a bit too conventional for me (I had begun to think "outside the box" in high school), I needed to join to show one and all by wearing their pin to prove I was wanted. These things did not help my lack of confidence. During this time my mother left my father and my grades really suffered. But she found that neither she nor society were ready for divorced women and she returned. However, I was feeling very alone and down. Just before my graduation I met a student on a blind date who was a veteran. He would eventually become my husband.

In the meantime I entered a graduate program in another university, becoming a registered occupational therapist. My first job was Director of Patient Services in a tuberculosis sanitarium. I had loved the course work but finally had to concede that working with suffering people triggered my depression just too much.

PART TWO

*"The longest journey is
the journey inwards."*

———————————

Dag Hammarskjold

NINE

Breaking Down or Through?

We have to be willing to get rid of the life we planned so
we can have the life that is waiting."

Joseph Campbell

My first nervous breakdown, or breakthrough, depending on one's
perspective, took place when I was twenty-nine. I had four active little
boys born in four and a half years, all single births; a husband who
was a workaholic and had developed a strong alliance with alcohol, (he
never drank at home so he was gone a lot); my father had died somewhat
unexpectedly so there was no chance for goodbyes; my mother was leaning
on me emotionally more than ever; there was my polio compromised body
and a tendency toward deep depression. Was it any wonder that I simply
could not get out of bed one morning?

I signed myself into the psychiatric unit of a hospital in a nearby city
where my mother had been a patient. My suicidal thoughts had returned
and suicide seemed like the sensible solution! (That's when it gets really
frightening!) However, my fierce love for my sons stopped me. I thought
of them as a sacred trust from God and I was not going to let anyone else
raise them!

One day at lunch another patient, Frances a French war bride, said to
me, "I think your leg is your problem." I quickly brushed her comment

off with, "Oh, no, that's all in the past." As it turned out, she knew better than the psychiatrist and the psychologist overseeing my case.

I did a very classic thing: I immediately fell in love with my psychologist. He was so kind, gentle and good natured, and his attention was focused just on me for an entire hour with no interruptions or distractions, three or four times a week. I could depend on that. He was never a "no show." This was a totally new experience for me and my first time in therapy

I was besotted!

Naturally my husband picked up on this and my psychologist had to sit him down and emphatically assure him that he was not going to divorce his wife and marry me. However, the attraction was emotional, not at all sexual. We never so much as shook hands when we met or when we said goodbye at the time of my discharge three weeks later. No longer seeing him was a major loss. I asked if I could have a yearly appointment with him, at least, and that's what we did for a long time. I mourned for him for nearly ten years and the pain was keen. That certainly spoke to the state of deprivation I was in. He and I were to exchange Christmas cards with notes for the next forty years, until his death. He was a dear man. May he rest in peace.

Returning home I relieved the relatives and hired woman who had been filling in for me during my absence. Sitting one afternoon on the top stairs of our quad-level house, it dawned on me for the first time that I could be *proactive,* that I could direct my life to a certain extent. So much had to been done *to* me by those around me in my childhood. This realization gave me a new sense of power! That moment was the beginning of my personal growth!

Another son (number five) was born to us which we anticipated with delight. Sadly he died soon after of viral pneumonia. I grieved long and hard. Expert John Schneider tells us that old unresolved grief is often triggered by new loss. That was definitely true in my case.

I decided to attend graduate school in psychology. I loved learning and I chose university classes over bridge and Junior League. That was my recreation. I also began working on Saturdays in an art gallery owned by a friend.

Our four sons grew and flourished. By the time they were well into their teenage years, they were all six foot four or six foot five. I did a lot of cooking; when I made French toast, I had to make forty-four pieces!

TEN

Getting Involved

"Never depend on governments or institutions to solve any problems. All social change comes from the passion of individuals."

Margaret Meade

By the time two of our sons were away in college and one in the Navy, I began taking courses toward a doctorate at Michigan State University. We lived near the campus. I was doing exceedingly well, according to my advising professor, when breakdown number two struck. I happened to be visiting a relative in Wisconsin and had to check in to a hospital there.

My depression was getting worse — a heavy, black, nauseating, crushing feeling that would flatten me like a steamroller. Even the smallest, most innocent thing would depress me. Sitting out on the hospital lawn one afternoon, a small plant with a single flower caught my attention. The symmetry of the petals and leaves, the delicate design and color, all helped assure me that there is a Supreme Intelligence behind everything from a flower to the human body to the planet and the solar system. My spirits began to lift.

Returning home, I read an article in our local newspaper describing the new medical problems many polio survivors were developing after years of stability. And, that a state-wide coalition of post-polios and health care professionals was forming, along with several human service agencies, to address these new problems and related issues. I signed up at once. I thought such work with such people would help alleviate my depression. I would be with kindred spirits — people who were veterans of the same "war." I could actually talk about polio with them and they would understand. It didn't quite work out that way.

Some of our meetings verged on group therapy. We needed to vent. We all had different priorities. There was a great deal of dissension. But, we soldiered on. After a year or so of meetings, the coalition incorporated into a 501 (c) (3) organization and I was asked to serve as the first Chairperson of the Board of Directors, just so a name could be put on the legal papers, but I found it so much to my liking that I continued in that position for the next two and a half years.

Simultaneously, I founded the first post-polio support group in Michigan and acted as facilitator. Coverage in the local newspaper of the formation of this support group and why brought phone calls the minute the paper hit the streets and lasted for three days. I kept a log and the calls totaled sixty plus. I lost my voice.

As a result, I was written up again in the local papers, I was on local radio and television. The news was picked up by the media across the country and I began getting phone calls from all over the country and even Hawaii, polio survivors who needed to talk!!

My mother said, "I don't see why you have to keep going over and over this! Couldn't you just be thankful polio wasn't any worse for you than it was and that your father could afford a good surgeon?" Guilt trip! The surgeon remark was a paper tiger — March of Dimes stepped in where there was financial need.

One Sunday after church, I was standing in the hallway through which the congregation was passing on the way to the social room for coffee. One of my mother's close friends stopped in front of me and said somewhat accusingly, "You know, your polio was really hard on your mother!" Surprising even me, I burst into angry tears right there in front of God and every one and shot back, "Why is it no one ever talks about what it was like for me! I'm the one who had polio!". She was speechless and hurriedly walked away. She didn't realize she was kicking a sleeping dog!

ELEVEN

Michigan Polio Network, Inc.

In addition to my duties as Chairperson, I did a fair amount of writing, speaking and other endeavors. I wrote Guidelines for Starting a Support Group For Polio Survivors, and then a humorous manual, with illustrations, called, How to Keep a Support Group Going Once It Began. I put together the twelve page report on a sixteen week psychotherapy group for post-polios, entitled "UNFINISHED BUSINESS, Support Group Members Confront Feelings Surrounding the Late Effects of Polio," (available on Facebook, on a closed site "Post Polio Coffee House," under Files). I appeared in a video of six post-polios discussing their experiences and feelings around polio and the late effects. This was made by the University of Michigan Medical Center. Another Board member, Sunny, and I conducted two one-day training workshops for new support group leaders from all over the state. She and I also co-authored a pamphlet on how to choose a personal counselor for those who had polio. I began speaking at state wide post-polio conferences in other parts of the country — Arizona, Connecticut, and Ohio. I was becoming a voice for the emotional/psychological damage of polio, which had been long overlooked And, I was having violent nightmares!

The dissension continued at our Board meetings and was becoming unmanageable for at least two of us. Sunny and I began writing a story about the Board members in the fairy tale idiom. I would write a paragraph and then send it to her. She would add to it and send it back to me. And so it went. It gave us a humorous relief; it was surprisingly effective!

One of the highlights for me in all of this was being asked to speak at an international conference in St. Louis, Missouri, which would be attended by 5-600 physicians and polio survivors from all over the United States and many foreign countries! I had become somewhat accustomed to public speaking by this time, but only somewhat. This would be huge! I wrote out and practiced carefully what I was going to say. The night before I was to give my ten minute talk (ten minutes is a long time when speaking before such an audience), I was up all night with a headache, nausea and nerves. I came to the conclusion I would just have to bow out. But, after some breakfast I changed my mind again. I did speak. I spoke about my favorite polio topic — the corresponding emotional/psychological damage of polio. I went so far as to suggest that one of the causes of the late effects we were experiencing might be old, unresolved emotional trauma of polio. That was a controversial thing to say, at the time. The speaker sitting next to me challenged that! She was a psychologist with a PhD. and I was a little intimidated. I hadn't planned on such an outright objection and I'm not so good at thinking of my feet. Besides, I was being videotaped. My reaction would become a permanent record and shown far and wide. However, a response came *through* me, not *from* me, and I calmly replied, "Well, let's see. How many polio survivors in the audience have noticed an improvement in their physical symptoms since having some psychotherapy, or know someone who has?" A significant number of hands went up!

I distributed twelve copies of the paper, 'UNFINISHED BUSINESS ..." at the same conference (twelve copies was all I could bring with me) to people from foreign countries only. To all others who gave me their names and address and one dollar to cover costs, in this country, I sent copies after returning home. I told every one they had my permission to copy and distribute all the copies they wished. I did not copyright it because I wanted to reach as many persons as possible. Eventually I had a collection of over seventy letters written to me in appreciation for the contents of the report This certainly pointed out the prevalence of old psychological damage that had never been resolved. No question.

I was taken by complete surprise when I attended a meeting arranged to honor me by naming me Alumnae of the Year for 1986-87 by the Office of Programs for Handicapper Students at Michigan State University!

TWELVE

Special Points of Interest

My husband and I had become friends with one particular polio victor and her husband. Judy was in a wheelchair, paralyzed from the neck down. She could sign her name, use a speaker phone and feed herself if everything was positioned properly for her. Her arms rested on shoulder-level supports that swiveled. She was on oxygen and had to sleep in an iron lung six nights a week. She hired someone to come in each morning, bathe and dress her and someone to come in and put her to bed at night. Eric was a wheelchair user, too, having been paralyzed from the waist down in a motorcycle accident.

We went to an outdoor shooting range with them. Formerly a machinist, Eric had designed and fabricated a special rifle for her when she told him she was a participator not a spectator. She could outshoot him!

One evening we all went out to dinner. I was dismayed to see the scowls on the faces of the other diners when Judy and Eric rolled in to the restaurant with all of Judy's apparatus. Many able-bodied persons feel threatened by others' handicaps. It must remind them that such things happen and could happen to them. There's a saying among handicappers I am fond of: "Handicappers are the only equal opportunity minority — anyone can join at any time."

During our dinner Judy asked me why I'd had so much emotional trauma around my polio saying, "But you can walk!" Her husband immediately came to my rescue asking, "Which is worse losing a big game by one or two points or by twenty-five or thirty?" I so appreciated that support! He said it so succinctly and quickly. In fact, Judy was much more well-adjusted than I. She'd had an entire year of rehabilitation (including psychological) in a large well-known hospital. I'd had none! Nor did those polio survivors like me.

This brings up the subject of non-severe disabilities. Russell Scabbo, PhD. did a study for his doctoral dissertation at Michigan State University and concluded that handicappers with non-severe disabilities suffer from unique stresses which had not before been identified: (1) Capacity for denial. (2) High expectation of performance from others. (3) Lack of belongingness in either the world of the able-bodied or that of the seriously handicapped. I was part of a group that had fallen through the cracks.

There was an interesting discussion at one of my support group meetings as to what we should call ourselves. Some members felt "polio survivor" was too grim, reminiscent of the Holocaust. "Polio victor" was another suggestion but that implied having been a victim. Frank proposed "persons who had had polio" because we are so much more than our polio. Very true, but that was lengthy and therefore probably wouldn't be used much. I leaned towards "polio thriver" but that hasn't caught on either.

During my time as Chairperson, the subject of "passing" came up: trying to pass as able-bodied. Jerry, whose non-dominant arm and hand were affected, kept that hand in his trouser pocket. No one would have guessed. Barbara who shoulders and arms were atrophied, wore jackets with custom-padded shoulders and short skirts which accented her lovely legs. I eventually wore pants or long skirts and long dresses. Why not? It makes us feel better.

In *The Dark Side of Camelot*, author Seymour Hersh writes that President John F. Kennedy was " ...sick or in pain most of his life, but rarely complained about it. That he was psychologically unable to do so. He was ashamed of his illnesses. He saw them as weaknesses." Sounds so familiar!

In his book, polio survivor and author Hugh Gallagher, writes in *F.D.R.'s Splendid Deception*, "A visible paralytic handicap affects every relationship, alters the attitudes of others, and challenges one's self-esteem. It requires meticulous minute-by-minute monitoring and control to an extent quite unperceived and unimaginable to the able-bodied. This condition of being handicapped generates a range of emotions, whether expressed or not, that must be dealt with not just at the onset, but continuing throughout the patient's life." If not attended to these feelings will likely smolder, fester and cast a shadow over every part of a post-polio's life.

Ann Kaiser Sterns advises in her book, *Living Through Personal Crises,* "You ... have to give up the idea that you aren't entitled to mourn because others have greater sorrows. All of us have both the right and the responsibility to take our losses seriously."

Back to Judy, her parents had been told by the doctors originally to put her in an instituition and forget her. She was just a "bag of bones." Well, Judy had other plans. She got an education and went on to organize and administer a prototype department for handling the needs of handicapper students at a Big Ten university. She married. She and Eric traveled, in a special van, arranging in advance with hospitals along the way for the overnight use of an iron lung. They became activists, advocating for handicappers. And, then they adopted a twelve year old girl, also a chair user. Unfortunately Judy is no longer with us, but her most inspiring spirit lives on and on!

THIRTEEN

Holistic Health

"Health is an inside job!"

Source unknown

Holistic medicine was beginning to interest me. I reviewed one of Deepak Chopra's early books, *Quantum Healing,* along with *Vibrational Medicine,* by Richard Gerber, M.D. in the support group newsletter that I had been putting out for several years. It did not go over well. It was considered witchcraft by some! I just couldn't interest polio survivors in that topic.

And, it seemed to me that our post-polio doctors were just preparing us for the late effects, rather than trying holistic methods to minimize, delay or prevent them. So I resigned as Chairperson of the Michigan Polio Network, Inc. and from my role in my support group, after two and a half years. (Ten years later holistic medicine was the subject of a statewide weekend long conference for post-polios in Michigan!)

August came and was terribly hot, I was quite tired and really shouldn't have spent the money, but I went anyway to a ten day residential workshop at a holistic health education center in southern Michigan and stayed for a year!! Going home on weekends.

I was exposed to many interesting people there and fascinating ideas about healing. The diet was vegetarian raw food, based on the work of Dr. Anne Wigmore. The center offered a two week program for those with serious illnesses (education not treatment) and for those who were well and wanted to stay that way. I learned so much. Working in the kitchen six hours a day, I earned my keep for the first six months, then was hired on staff to teach classes on creating our own health, some of which I designed. Early onset cataracts ended my ability to commute any longer and I left with real regret one year to the day I first arrived.

*   *   *

The morning after my husband's second DWI arrest, he announced that he liked drinking and was not going to stop! Our sons were grown and gone. It was time for me to go. The problems created by his behavior were taking a serious toll on my health. I had to conclude that just because two people love each other, it doesn't necessarily mean they should be together.

The business of leaving that life was long, complex and it hurt! Badly! I had no way of knowing if I could make it on my own, but I had to try! As author Erica Jong said, "To risk nothing is to risk everything." (I'm sure she didn't mean foolish risks.) I knew I'd rather try and fail than not try at all. It did help that I had something in mind to go *to,* that had been calling me for a long time and that was Santa Fe, New Mexico.

FOURTEEN

Santa Fe, New Mexico

Santa Fe, New Mexico was all that I had longed for and more! It fed me, mind, body and soul. Located in the southern end of the Rocky Mountains at an altitude of 7,000 feet, in what is known as high desert, it has four seasons and a very dry climate. The horizon is wide open with an ever changing sky and gorgeous sunsets. There are juniper, piñon and other green trees, lilacs and tulips in the spring.

Three cultures coexist, a little uneasily at times: Anglo, Native American and Hispanic. I've always been drawn to anything Native American, but I was especially drawn to the Hispanic; the mariachi bands, the flamenco dancers, the festivals all exuded a passion for life. A real contrast to the uptight, conformist, cerebral community I had lived in until then. It allowed a person to be an individual. Even those from the Pleides.

In addition, Santa Fe has five colleges and universities, the five major religions, countless art galleries, an internationally known opera house, and numerous healing modalities, plus restaurants of all kinds.

I lived in Santa Fe and environs for close to twenty years, having many grand adventures. To name a few, I met a middle-aged, educated, activist couple who later invited me to travel with them, their newborn son and Appaloosa horse, on the roads and streets of California living with the homeless for six weeks. (That is to be another book.) I wrote for a newspaper with international distribution, book reviews and interviews, that only carried good news, major good news, not puppies in baskets.

I designed, built and decorated a straw-bale house in the mountains, wanting to have a Walden Pond experience. Just after beginning this project, I was diagnosed with CFS, Chronic Fatigue Syndrome, caused in my case by a common virus to which most people are immune. I felt pretty awful for several years. I also remarried during this time. Any of those three things — illness, building a house, marrying — are high on the stress scale, but I hardly hesitated to do all three at the same time, being the Type A post-polio that I was.

A Catholic parish priest, Fr. Pretto was an accomplished pianist and vocalist, from Panama who played salsa music every Friday night for dancing, as part of his ministry. He was one of those legends in his own time. I had a passion for dancing I had never been able to explore.

Polio had left me with feet of different sizes, necessitating the purchase of two pair every time I bought shoes. Finding the same style, the same color, in the same store at the same time was not easy. My feet were a housing problem! Just prior to leaving Michigan, I had happened across a shoemaker who custom made some over the ankle boots with a soft soles that laced up snuggly, for me. The soft sole permitted better balance, my toes could "grab" the floor. I had also purchased some knee-high Minnetonka moccasins. I had to buy two pair, but since they didn't have a right or a left to them, I could switch the sizes and still have two pair. These boots were made for dancing! Long skirts were very much in style, so I appeared able-bodied. I danced! I couldn't do any fancy footwork but I learned to excel in graceful upper body movements, receiving compliments from friends and strangers. I didn't care who was looking at me I was going to dance! It wasn't necessary to have a partner for salsa dancing — people danced alone, in pairs or in groups. The building would actually vibrate as the music and the dancers celebrated the end of the week and celebrated being alive! Those were great times!

I also went dancing at a local hotel with a friend who understood and anticipated my limits. With his help, I learned the Texas two-step. Thanks, Bill, wherever you may be! There was another dancing venue I attended called the Body Choir, held twice a week in a dance studio. Participants came to dance out their feelings, be they sad, joyful, angry or thankful. Every one danced solo and no talking was allowed, except during the break. Slow, recorded music began the evening and gradually accelerated over the course of the two hours. Everyone danced in bare feet or socks to protect the expensive floor, but I was granted permission to wear my softsoled boots as I couldn't have danced otherwise. It was in every respect a wonderful workout.

I danced my heart out for the better part of seven years and I had moments of euphoria. It all came to an end when I moved out into the mountains. It was just too long a drive back after a rigorous evening of dancing.

My dancing today is pretty much out of the question as I have an AFO (ankle foot orthotic) and use a walker. (Because of the AFO I now only need to buy one pair of shoes!!) I do dance occasionally, sitting in a chair. I've never minded that I couldn't play tennis, or other ball sports, but I do grieve not being a polished, versatile dancer, dancing the tango, for instance. The tango is the most sensual, sophisticated, disciplined activity I have ever witnessed. Ever! I really hope that reincarnation turns out to be the case as I want an entire lifetime of accomplished dancing.

My second husband and I had been married and living out in the mountains for several years when our marriage exploded, after such a promising beginning, with seismic repercussions for me, shaking me to my depths, and finally releasing the issues of abandonment and separation anxiety from my polio experience. He left and I was diagnosed with PTSD. Another hospitalization followed during which enormous rage surfaced. I couldn't believe I was even capable of such rage! It was so innervating. I felt as though I could run right up the sides of skyscrapers and leap from one building top to another! And it lasted for days. Plus, I cried a major waterfall of tears.

Eventually I sold my house, my dream house, as living in a "back to nature" lifestyle alone in the mountains was way too physically demanding for me. I moved back to Santa Fe.

*   *   *

Post Traumatic Stress Disorder was identified first in veterans of the Vietnam War and probably called shell-shock prior to that. I have experienced most all the symptoms at one time or another: nightmares, flashbacks, startle reflex, over commitment to distract oneself, indecisiveness, paranoia, emotional numbness, guilt, shame, sadness, hyper vigilance and of course depression and anxiety. It takes a lot of time and effort to overcome PTSD. Actually, it's more a matter of management rather than cure.

My life in the "Land of Enchantment," as New Mexico is known, included two more volunteer hospitalizations for the Ogre depression. The negative thoughts that run through the mind of someone with acute depression are often intolerable. My anxiety became severe and was so strong I had to pace the floor, I was unable to sleep much at all, and couldn't swallow more than a couple of mouthfuls of food per day. I rapidly lost weight.

It is with great hesitation that I disclose the fact that I have needed hospitalization for depression and anxiety a total of SIX times in my adult life. Not even my close friends know that number. It made me feel very defective, plus I worried that people would assume I was crazy or even dangerous. I was neither. I was hurting! And, I was ASHAMED! There's still a stigma around mental illness, even though that is improving. But, with my history I wonder if I would be able to purchase a gun or run for public office. Not that I'm thinking of doing either.

FIFTEEN

Psychiatric Units and Psychotherapists

Psychiatric units in hospitals are not fun places. Not a Doris Day kind of experience, but some are much better than others. There can be some very disturbed patients with shocking stories. And some of the psychotherapists (psychiatrists and psychologists) can be angels, so helpful, but others unethical, or still working out their own personal problems. (This is also true of therapists in private practice.) It's best to stay out of these units if at all possible. If not, they do provide short-term care for a person when they can't take care of themselves, and they keep a patient safe from self-harming (cutting, burning and suicide.)

In one psychiatric unit, my only roommate in a four-bed room insisted on keeping the window blinds closed during the day because she was certain the Texas Rangers were looking for her. One morning she awoke to find a large black feather lying on the floor at the foot of her bed and she went berserk, crying and shaking! She knew it had been put there by a Satanic cult! A nurse rushed in to see what all the commotion was about and the nurse shrieked, "Oh, my god! That's gang writing," pointing to chalked symbols on one of the bare mattresses. That set my roommate off on another tirade.

One day later on in that same unit, a female patient threatened to "rip the head off" an another female patient. It was a holiday weekend and the unit was short staffed. No one was in the nurses station at the time. Another patient came to the rescue and gently defused the situation. The aggressor went to her room and burned a large crucifix on her forearm with a cigarette. There were no consequences for her, even though that behavior, burning, was expressly forbidden There were many worse things I either witnessed or endured. Horrible things! I could write a book about just that.

SIXTEEN

Falling!

London bridges falling down had nothing on me. Falling became a regular happening as soon as I was able to discard my brace, about the end of eighth grade. The days of spontaneous movements were over. I needed to survey the terrain as if I were looking for land mines. The smallest thing could trip me, a pebble, the edge of a sidewalk, a rug. This was the case for years, but I put off getting an AFO (ankle foot orthotic) as long as I possibly could, as long as seventeen years after Dr. Fred Maynard suggested I get one! I waited until my aging drop-foot began dragging and I had no other choice. In the meantime I'd had years of falls and my knees took a lot of punishment, as well as my pride. When I finally did give in, I wished I'd done it sooner. It eliminated my limp and did away with most of my falls. Eventually I also needed a cane, but I didn't mind. I had an assortment of attractive ones.

The day after Christmas, 2011, I fell and broke my polio hip, or my hip broke and then I fell … I'm not sure which. I was simply standing beside my bed when it happened. My hip had to be replaced. I had an excellent surgeon, had almost no post-op pain, and the incision nearly invisible.

During rehab, I was pushed by the physical therapist more than I should have been, but none of us knew any better then. An electric wheelchair was prescribed and custom-made to my dimensions, as I would be moving into a senior residence with very long hallways. Well, I wasn't having that wheelchair!! I learned quickly to use a walker, employing the wheelchair only when absolutely necessary. There were too many childhood memories of wheelchairs. I felt ashamed in one. An invalid, in-valid.

In Richard L. Bruno, HD, PhD.'s book, mentioned earlier, he cites a post-polio patient who said he'd rather commit suicide than use a cane! That's just the way we are. We want to be and look as able-bodied as we can.

SEVENTEEN

Insights

"Until the subconscious becomes conscious it will direct our lives and we will call it fate."

Carl Jung

I used to picture myself as an irregular city skyline— tall buildings randomly mixed with short buildings, sort of a vertical bar graph, symbolizing the ways in which I was more mature than my peers and in other ways less mature. Or a patchwork quilt, having various abilities and experiences, fastened together in a haphazard fashion. Along with a hollow core in the center of my being. In other words, I was not at all "homogenized," if you will.

I had become a perfectionist as I believed I had to be perfect to be loved. And I expected perfection from others. I was inwardly critical and judgmental, although I took great pains not to let it show. I disliked that in myself and it set me up for a lot of frustration. Anne Lamott, author, says perfectionism is an oppressor. Yes, indeed!

Putting a spin on bad situations was something I had become adept at; it had become second nature. While I fooled others, I fooled myself as well. I had great difficulty seeing red flags. I'm sure that dates back to, "We're going to pretend this all (polio) never happened."

Rather late in life I realized I've had a real penchant for emotionally wounded men. The more wounded the better! These men also had many positive qualities, but they were definitely wounded. As soon as a potential sweetheart revealed his wound(s), I was hooked! I knew what his pain felt like and I couldn't bear it. I had to help him because I knew what it felt like not to be helped. I would heal him with love, make it all better, bring him back to emotional health. (I think I was trying to heal my wounded inner child in the process.) We would understand each other in ways an emotionally healthy partner couldn't. Only it didn't work. Neither of us became healed. Then I became addicted to trying to get something from him he just didn't have to give. I married two of these men. But now that I understand what I was really doing, I won't do it again. There's already been a "test case" — a relationship which I backed out of early on. I'm not even tempted!

Today my personality feels more blended, coordinated. The hollow core has been filled. I'm still working on the perfection thing. Making progress. I simply don't have the energy to be or do perfect anymore. I shy away from red flags, even pink ones. I dislike cliches and try my best not to use them, but sometimes they say it so well, as in I finally "got it together." At least enough.

One of my spiritual teachers of many years, Michael Ryce, holds doctorates in both Holistic Philosophy and Naturopathic Medicine, and has a healing center in the Ozark Mountains. He has written a book called, *Why Is This Happening to Me ... AGAIN?* It explains that until we recognize our dysfunctional patterns and correct the cause, we are bound to repeat them over and over and over, until we do understand what we're doing.

Psychiatrist Viktor Frankl puts it this way, 'It's never to late to learn— but neither is it too soon; it is always "high time" we learned whatever is to be learned.'

EIGHTEEN

Joyous

"I never knew broken glass could shine so brightly."

Leonard Bernstein's *MASS*

I am overjoyed to say that it has been nearly fourteen years since my last episode of clinical depression and anxiety. I haven't even come close! I've been able to gradually taper down from a serious "cocktail" of five psychotropic medications, to just one and have remained on just that one for over three years now. Chances are I will always need it. I no longer have the constant, low level hum of inner turmoil which was so distracting. And I no longer weep over polio as I once predicted in my short poem at the beginning of Chapter Two.

I have a sense of confidence and inner peace that I never had before. That's not to say I don't get upset over life's problems, but underneath is a solid foundation now. I finally feel free to be truly happy. I am more of the person I always wanted to be! THIS IS VERY BIG!

It has taken many years and many things to accomplish this, such as: lots and lots of psychotherapy from many different therapists; medication when appropriate; attendance at numerous personal growth lectures and workshops; participation in a variety of support groups; graduate studies in psychology; countless self-help books; along with spiritually oriented study and discussion groups.

Having been raised in the Christian tradition, a Protestant denomination, I expanded my reading to include the other major world religions. I have been like Ravi Ravindra, PhD., who states in his book, *Christ* The *Yogi, A Hindu Reflection on The Gospel of John,* "I'll take the light wherever I can." I find that all the major world religions, and some indigenous ones, have something of value to offer. They differ in their emphasis.

Every morning I lie in bed for an hour or more before getting up for the day. During this time I pray, appreciate, ponder, wonder, reminisce, speculate, anticipate, problem-solve, question and fantasize. Contemplation is said to be the highest form of activity; not being constantly busy and on the go. Productivity is highly valued in the West, where as in the East stillness, and meditation are valued more. Some of my most creative ideas, remarkable insights and solutions come to me during these first morning hours.

*   *   *

I've done a fair amount of freelance writing over the year for magazines and newspapers. Along with newsletters. About two and a half years ago an inner force began demanding that I write down my polio story, as a sort of self-validation. This force was so insistent I couldn't ignore it; I simply had to do it. I thought my descendants might find it interesting, and then it occurred to me that my story could be helpful to other polio survivors, their families and friends, and possibly to families of children who have suffered other major illnesses or permanent injuries. And, so began this book.

To my surprise, after writing for a few hours, I would begin to feel nauseated and fearful with a repugnancy for anything to do with polio, followed by a firm decision to give up the whole project. In time these feelings would fade and I'd begin writing again with enthusiasm. This happened over and over. It was wearing me down. I tried several ways to conquer this disruptive pattern, but to no avail.

By now I was quite committed to this project and the solution seemed to be consulting a psychologist. The perfect therapist just fell into my lap the same day! My guardian angel must have had a hand in that. Dr. Molden specializes in seniors and in trauma, and has had nearly forty years of experience. After one or two sessions she said, "Sounds like you have PTSD."! Going back over my life had stirred up the remnants of that disorder. This time I believed it! It made sense of so many things in my past that I had thought were due to my sensitive nature, or some awful congenital defect. The two of us devised a strategy to combat those interruptions in my writing and they gradually decreased significantly. I still have nightmares, but perhaps they will cease when I finish this manuscript.

EPILOGUE

So often I hear people speak of wanting to put closure on a significant loss. I'm not sure that's even possible. What happened, happened. It has changed us. It's part of who we are now, who we have become. What we CAN do is change our perspective on the loss. Maybe not completely, but enough that we can go on.

The most surprising thing I have learned in my journey to inner healing is this:

Happiness Can Be Retroactive!

And, I conclude:

We Are Much More Than Our Bodies!

We are eternal spirits!

FAIRY TALES

THE LITTLE LAME PRINCESS

Once upon a time, not so long ago nor far away, there was a little lame princess, one of the fairest in the land, who lived with the Fire King and the Dwarf Queen. When she was of tender age, a plague descended upon the realm, spreading fear and destruction everywhere. When it lifted, the little princess could walk no more and it took many seasons before she could. The Fire King and the Dwarf Queen gave her fine gowns, lessons in the arts, and took her on pilgrimages to distant places. But, what she wished for, more than anything, was to be once more like other young maidens in the land! She wanted to run through the meadows and dance at the balls, to wear satin slippers and to laugh!

But, alas, an evil spell had fallen upon the castle. None could speak of her illness or her wishes! When they thought to do so, their very hearts stopped beating and their tongues froze in their mouths. Although the Fire King and the Dwarf Queen ruled the castle, they did not have the power to break this spell.

The years passed and the little lame princess, who was called Witherina, saddened and sickened. She banished all the looking-glasses from the Kingdom. She kept to her bedchamber. She thought she would surely die of her heartbreak. All the wise Councilors agreed that an enchanted Spindle would restore the little lame princess to health.

In time, Witherina found a fine Spindle which suited her fancy, and she closed herself into the tower to spin. Together, she and the Spindle spun some good things, but alas, alack ... the Spindle was not enchanted! In fact, it was tragically flawed. The evil spell continued and none could speak of her wishes, the very thing that was making her mortally ill.

The Fire King died and the old Dwarf Queen continued to rule from her weaknesses, which were most potent. The royal pair had been devoted to Witherina, but could not comprehend her malady. Their vision was limited. The Fire King had his own torment, pursued by a faceless demon; the Dwarf Queen suffered from a strange effect which had arrested her growth in childhood.

Then one day, there appeared a Fairy Godmother named Therapina. There had been other Fairy Godmothers, but they had lacked magic wands. Therapina spoke to Witherina thus, "Come let us weep together, so that you may smile. Let us rage together against the heavens so that you may know tranquility. Let us examine what is gone so that we may see what remains."

Witherina and Therapina talked and wept, talk and raged, and the evil spell began to shatter. Wondrous things happened. The meadows and the balls, the slippers and the laughter came closer to Witherina. She shifted and reach out to them. She found a pair of magical red boots which were followed by boots of many colors. She went to the balls and learned to move with gentle grace and confidence, often transported. She changed her name to Edifyna.

And, so, the little lame princess became a tall Queen, who just happened to be lame, and she went forth to live in dignity, wisdom and joy … and sometimes mischief!

Charlene Elizabeth
March 1985

THE GIRL WHO HAD NO SKIN

A story about the necessity of validation.

Once upon a time there was a girl who had no skin. She hurt, ever so much! She had no protection against life's slings and arrows. She could not bear even the gaze of others. Her night dreams were filled with danger, confusion and helplessness. Because of all these things she would writhe and moan, day and night.

For years, this girl who had no skin, wandered in the darkest part of the forest in hiding. That gave her some respite, yet it was so lonely there. On occasion she did venture out, very much on guard. She would hunch her shoulders and wrap her long, slender arms about herself. In this way, she strove to fortify herself against attack, abandonment and disregard. What she dreaded most was being misunderstood. She would return to the forest from these encounters with others, disheartened and exhausted, this girl who had no skin.

One day she came upon a faint path through the gnarled and ancient trees, one she had not seen before. Treading along its winding way she found herself in a clearing, surrounded by a circle of bright mirrors. She saw herself from all sides at one time. The mirrors sang to her gently and truthfully. They told her she was indeed good, kind and worthwhile, that she was strong and had creative powers.

This girl who had no skin stood straight and tall, spreading her arms in joy! Strange sensations made her realize she was at last growing a skin. She looked upon her body and was astounded to see feathers forming. She spread her wings and began to fly. And she flew from star to star to star, this girl who once upon a time had no skin,

Charlene Elizabeth
September 1996

ABOUT THE AUTHOR

A polio survivor herself, Charlene Elizabeth became involved in the post-polio movement in the early 1980's when polio survivors were developing new medical problems after years of stability. She served as the first Chairperson of the Board of the Michigan Polio Network, Inc. for two and a half years while founding and facilitating the first support group in Michigan for polio survivors. She was named Alumnae of the Year for 1986-87 by the Office of Programs for Handicapper Students at Michigan State University.

Charlene graduated from Stephens College in Columbia, Missouri with Honors in Masterpieces of World Literature, from Michigan State University with a bachelor's degree in Textiles, Clothing, and Related Arts, and from Western Michigan University as a Registered Occupational Therapist. She has also done graduate work in psychology and is a freelance writer.

She is the proud mother of five sons, and a grandmother of eight. Currently she resides in North Carolina.

Your responses are welcome at c.elizabeth1960@gmail.com

Made in the USA
Coppell, TX
21 November 2020

41808722R10042